Growing & Using Scented Geraniums

by

Mary Peddie

Judy Lewis

John Lewis

How the Scenteds Came to Our Gardens

The popularity of the scented geraniums is well deserved. They are gregarious plants, mixing happily in the garden with one another or with other plants. They are excellent container specimens, and quite amenable to indoor life. For the most part the flowers are modest and unassuming: it is the varied textures and scented leaves of these plants that continue to charm gardeners worldwide, just as they fascinated Europeans who discovered them in South Africa in the early 1600s.

Certainly nothing like them existed in Europe, and it must have been with great glee that they were received and propagated. They were quickly identified as belonging to the Family Geraniaceae and became the "scented geraniums." A century later, when Linnaeus, the great Swedish botanist, brought order to our understanding of the plant world, the Geraniaceae Family was divided into three genera — the true *Geraniums*, the *Erodiums*, and the *Pelargoniums* — and the scenteds were more correctly identified as pelargoniums.

The pelargoniums number more than 280 species and subspecies, mostly native to South Africa. Of this number perhaps 30 species are cultivated as scented-leaf geraniums. But they have crossed with one another and with other species of pelargoniums to produce a bewildering range of cultivars. There are brothers and half-brothers, cousins and half-cousins.

But to this day, the bright, continuously blooming common pelargonium — a colorful addition to any window box — and its cousin, the fragrant-leafed plant, are incorrectly dubbed "geraniums." Gardeners in England, New Zealand, Australia, and South Africa speak of pelargoniums, but here in the United States we recognize them as geraniums. As we become more knowledgeable and sophisticated about our gardening, perhaps we, too, will someday correctly refer to them as the "scented pelargoniums."

The seventeenth and eighteenth centuries were marked by expansion and adventure. Nearly every great voyage of discovery had a plantsman, or at least a learned man, aboard to observe and collect examples of the flora and fauna of strange lands. These voyages were commercial ventures; plants, sought for their medicinal properties, were profitable acquisitions. Certainly these unusual plants, which mimicked so many other known plants, must have some curative properties! And so it was that the scented geraniums found places of honor in the great botanical collections of the day.

Because they were easily propagated and their scents so unusual, the scenteds quickly became popular subjects for all types of gardens throughout Europe. They were found in both the great manor house orangeries and in cottage gardens. Although perennial in their native habitat, they could be successfully wintered over in northern Europe. Many survived on a cottage windowsill. This ability to withstand rigorous treatment made them well traveled and universally loved. They came to North America with the earliest settlers, and by 1790 colonial plantsmen listed some twenty varieties.

Lore and Facts

It was not until the medical world accepted the reclassification of these plants as pelargoniums that the search for medicinal properties ceased. A few of the pelargoniums did have some uses medicinally, but these were not the species we now classify as having a scented leaf. However, the scenteds continued to be associated with herbs.

Because they smelled like certain foods, some of them began to be used in cooking by 1818. The rose geranium was added to jelly, and some stalwart soul, who had probably been to Turkey, even began making a rose geranium syrup similar to the attar of rose syrup used on sweets in the Turkish courts. But for the most part the leaves were used in potpourri and in sleep pillows. Between 1800 and the 1890s only a few new scenteds appeared, most of which were deliberately hybridized in botanic gardens in Europe.

It was the Victorians, with their lush houseplants and lavish gardens, who truly began to confuse us about the scented geraniums. Growers of the late 1890s listed dozens of varieties, yet descriptions of many of these were quite similar. Apparently some crosses and recrosses occurred naturally, but much hybridization was deliberate and growers arbitrarily named cultivars as they pleased. Some growers attempted to define the hybrid, but many simply tacked on a saleable name (and are apt to do so today) and introduced a "new" geranium. Even using modern techniques, we will never be able to classify precisely all the scented pelargoniums now sold.

In the 1940s a group met in New England to discuss this problem and concluded that the best way to bring a modicum of order to the situation was to classify them by scent. In this, we use three criteria: first the scent; second the leaf shape, foliage color, and texture; and lastly the flower shape, color, and reproductive parts.

But another variable enters into this fact finding: how and where a geranium is grown. Garden plants exhibit growth patterns and coloration that may not be so outstanding in a container-grown plant. And sometimes the neat container-grown plant bears little resemblance to the rampant brother in the garden. Different soils produce oblique differences in the very same plant. The best we can do is give some general outlines and let gardeners have the fun of deciding which scented is growing in their garden or on their patio.

One bit of lore needs to be refuted. Occasionally someone in the greenhouse says, "Oh, the scented geraniums — I don't grow them because they are poisonous!" We have tried unsuccessfully to find the source of this idea. They are not poisonous — at least not in the uses we make of them. We do not know if they could be used for grazing cattle, but the flowers, leaves, and extracts have all been used for centuries.

General Classifications

The following descriptions are general, but they should help you to identify the plants you grow. Today there are probably more than 200 different scented geraniums available, and over a hundred more that have surreptitiously crept into the category. This includes flowering types, such as the Unique pelargoniums, and those with distinctive leaf shapes, like the grape-leaved pelargonium. Those we list in this book are true scenteds, with distinctive and individual aromas.

The Rose-Scented Pelargoniums

This is the largest and most beloved group of scented geraniums. There are two distinct leaf patterns, both triangular, in this group. One is more or less lobed; botanically it is *Pelargonium capitatum*.

The other pattern is deeply cut and, in fact, may be quite open. This is *P. graveolens*, from which most of the hybrids have been developed. However, the crossovers are so numerous and so ancient it is impossible to distinguish all of them.

The Mint-Scented Pelargoniums

Here we have an easily identified group. The mint or peppermint geranium has a large, hirsuit (fuzzy) leaf and is named *P. tomentosum* because of its wooly texture. It has the habit of spreading exuberantly, and is one of the few scenteds which require mottled shade for optimum growth. Although few in number, the mint geraniums are a valuable addition to any collection. Mint has been crossed with others to produce deeply lobed leaves with dark centers.

The Fruit-Scented Pelargoniums

There are several distinct fruit types. Citrus is the largest group and contains many long-recognized citrus varieties. One, a hybrid of ancient origin, *P.* x *nervosum*, is the lime geranium, which truly does smell like limes. The 'Mabel Grey', introduced to the United States in 1973, is more lemony than lemons. Most of the citrus varieties are distinctly shrubby, with serrated leaves. Some have dark green leaves; others such as the 'Mabel Grey', are a light green. Variegated citrus scenteds, such as 'French Lace', have been grown for more than a hundred years.

Other fruit-scented types may have only one or two varieties or cultivars in each category. The apple, or *P. odoratissimum*, meaning very fragrant, is exactly that. True apple geraniums simply smell like fresh apples. All of the fruit-scented types seem to hybridize readily, and there are a number of charming offspring, including two different strains of Old Spice: one is more like the apple, the other has the grey cast of a nutmeg.

The Pungent-Scented Geraniums

Most of the plants in this group belong to, or are closely related to, the *P. quercifolium* or oak-leaf-shaped group. Some growers note a eucalyptus scent, others think of them as pine, and indeed, our experience has been that these and other sharp scents may be quite clearly detected in selected plants. Some gardeners may find the pungent group more pungent than pleasant. Many have quite distinct coloration on the leaf and bloom profusely, and thus deserve a place in the garden. The *quercifolium* species hybridizes easily, even with geraniums that are not considered scenteds. The results are interesting and vigorous, but not necessarily sweet-smelling.

Spice-Scented Pelargoniums

This classification has relatively few members but is exemplified by the long recognized *P. fragrans*, or nutmeg geranium. Others, such as 'Cinnamon Rose' with its spicy rose scent, may be placed in this category or left in the rose group, since the leaves more closely resemble that parentage. Ginger, *P.* x *nervosum* 'Toronto', is frequently classified as *P. torento*, but this has no botanical standing. New cultivars, such as 'Apple Cider', are definitely spicy, and regardless of leaf shape, color, or texture, belong in the spice group.

Others

Of course there are others — scented-leaf cultivars or species that defy classification. In the past few years it has been customary for some growers to include the pelargoniums known in England as the Uniques as scenteds. This is a dubious addition, for the foliage may be only slightly pleasant. Like the common zonal geranium, the foliage may well be odoriferous! However, these plants cross with many of the species in the scented group and do have quite distinctive blossoms, a desirable attribute.

Thus it is obvious that much depends on a specific plant and the eye of the beholder. And when it comes to classification of the scenteds by our sense of smell, the matter becomes most subjective.

Scenteds in the Garden

As natives of the temperate regions, pelargoniums require warmth and good drainage, but in many countries they thrive in a variety of soils. Generally they prefer full sun (in the Sun Belt shield them from the afternoon sun), but many tolerate partial shade. Only the mint geraniums, the old *P. tomentosum* and the newer *P. tomentosum* 'Chocolate Mint', require shade. They make a wonderful groundcover around an established tree. 'Pungent Peppermint' and 'Joy Lucille' are much more tolerant of the sun.

For best results in a garden of scenteds we recommend soil amendments, fertilizers, and plant food.

Often these terms are used interchangeably, but the primary use of a soil amendment is to change the basic character of a soil, to make it more porous, more alkaline, or more water-retentive. Fertilizers provide nutrients for a plant, but these are not all readily available and sometimes must be broken down even further before they can be absorbed by the plant. A plant food, usually applied as a water-soluble chemical compound, feeds the plant immediately.

Some products may do all three, but plant food, for example, ordinarily is consumed by the plant and does not alter the soil. Sometimes a water-soluble compound is labeled "fertilizer" when in the strictest sense it is only a plant food.

Transplanting Outdoors

To transplant a 6-inch potted geranium in the garden, dig a hole 12 inches deep and about 9 inches across. Add soil amendments as necessary. In sandy soil place a 1-inch layer of peat moss at the bottom of the hole. In clay soil place a 3-inch layer of sand for drainage. Set plant in place, loosening the roots from the root ball as necessary. Fill hole with good topsoil. Water well, but water the soil, not the foliage of the plant. As a rule, scented geraniums do not like to get their leaves wet.

Large plants in the garden benefit from a top dressing of mulch, but it should be of a porous material, which does not stay damp. Cedar, eucalyptus, and pine bark are good organic mulches available commercially. Rock, gravel, sand, and products such as Turface are attractive inorganic materials.

Watering

Geraniums are best watered with a soaker hose. Only in very dry areas is an occasional sprayer application of water needed. In their native habitat the pelargoniums are often found in small patches of soil between rocky outcroppings. The large fleshy roots can grow to several feet in a single summer, and will eagerly seek water and nourishment. When watering, it is best to give the scenteds a deep watering, rather than a sprinkle on top. They have few small feeder roots on the surface.

Hints for Bigger and Better Plants

Soil amendments, fertilizers, and plant foods produce large, showy plants in one season. Ideal soil contains plant nutrients and holds some moisture, but drains well, permitting oxygen to permeate the interstices between soil particles. Clay soils, although difficult for the gardener, often contain many nutrients that are released under favorable conditions. They can be amended with gypsum and humus. Sandy soils do not contain enough nutrients and need to be amended with humus, peat, or compost, but provide good drainage. Plants in sandy soils require regular fertilization and an occasional plant food application. In a good rich loam, fertilization may not be required during the entire growing season.

In such a rich soil, an application of iron chelate in mid-August gives plants that are to be brought indoors an extra boost. Cuttings taken about three weeks after an application of iron chelate will root well and produce nice small plants for a windowsill. In those parts of the country where the scenteds grow all year, some fertilization is required to maintain healthy plants, especially if they are being cut regularly or require water frequently. Frequent watering leaches nutrients from the soil.

In a sandy soil fertilize every thirty days with a general-purpose fertilizer. It is wise to alternate the types of fertilizers and plant foods by using (1) fish emulsion, (2) a water-soluble chemical combination, or (3) an organic fertilizer such as dehydrated manure. Read the label carefully. To induce more blooms, decrease the amount of nitrogen in the fertilizer.

Container-grown geraniums thrive on a variety of fertilizers and plant foods; but again, alternate the types used. A 5-10-10 or similar formula is a safe combination. Do not overfertilize, but if you have to water frequently, remember that the water is leaching away plant nutrients, which must be replaced. An application of one of the timed-release fertilizers is good insurance. Several good brands are available at garden centers.

It takes about fifteen weeks for bloom buds to form in the tips of the scented geraniums. If you want to enjoy blossoms, do not pinch severely. To keep plants healthy and sturdy indoors during the winter, they must receive a lot of light. A south window with supplemental light insures growth, and a fan moving air over them makes them branch and stay stocky. The scenteds thrive indoors; part of this may be due to the reduced humidity found in most homes. They do not tolerate misting or high humidity often required for tropical houseplants.

Pests and Diseases

The scenteds are robust plants, occasionally subject to mealybugs, whiteflies, and, infrequently, red spider mites or leaf miners. In the garden these insects rarely cause a great deal of damage. You will find the scenteds are "home base" for praying mantises, who do their part in making off with injurious insects.

Indoors, pests invariably find the sweetest-smelling of any collection. Apparently insects enjoy them as much as we! Use any insecticidal soap or a chemical houseplant insecticide; read and follow directions carefully. Stem damage, overwatering, and cold encourage disease. In midwinter move plants to a sunny window where they will get good and ample light; see that they have good ventilation. Water sparingly.

Fungus and virus infections are uncommon but possible. If stems become soft and dark, or leaves wilt and look dull, isolate the plant. Repot in fresh growing medium and cut back all damaged parts. Sterilize clippers after use. Do not attempt to take cuttings from an infected plant.

If a plant does not put out vigorous new growth, discard plant and soil. Sterilize the pot in a 20 percent chlorine solution before reusing.

Twelve Wonderful Plants to Grow

For a summary of plant characteristics, refer to the chart at the back of this bulletin.

P. x *capitatum* 'Attar of Rose'

This popular rose scented acquires some of its popularity because of the romantic name. Not all 'Attar of Rose' strains are heavily scented. This cultivar was once thought to have been introduced commercially for oil extraction to replace the rare true rose extract from Turkey. However, no record of it exists before 1907, when it was introduced to the trade in Britain by Cannel and Sons, a popular nursery operation closely allied to Kew Gardens. It is very similar to the *P. capitatum*, which was probably the source of the oil. *P. capitatum* is a fast-growing plant with weak and trailing stems. This cultivar is a slightly compact plant that is branched and has tri-lobed leaves, gently notched and somewhat light green in color. One strain has pink flowers; another produces a more lavender shade.

Select a vigorous, strong-scented 'Attar of Rose'. It is an excellent garden plant, likes full sun, and can stand a good deal of aridity. As a houseplant it requires abundant sun but infrequent watering. In midwinter it tends to become "leggy" and does best if pinched back severely in early fall.

P. x *graveolens* 'Grey Lady Plymouth'

'Grey Lady Plymouth' displays a pencil-thin line of creamy white about the border of its sage green leaves. It is quite fragrant, and its deeply lobed leaves add much interest to the garden. The 'Lady Plymouth', its sister plant, is quite similar but boasts a wider margin of creamy white on the leaves, which are more a true green and have a slightly less pronounced scent.

This is a very adaptable houseplant. In confinement it seldom grows to more than 18 inches and maintains its compact size under most light conditions. A look-alike plant is the silver-edged rose, which is quite grey in color but does not evidence the line of white around the leaves. Some cultivars have pink flowers, others tend toward lavender hues.

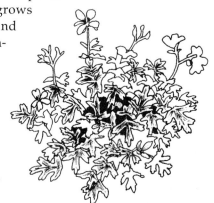

P. x *graveolens* and *P.* x *jatropholium* 'Rober's Lemon Rose'

Introduced by Ernest Rober in the 1930s, this old-time favorite has leaves that look like those of a tomato plant. It is bushy, and the irregularly lobed leaves are rather thick. It grows upright, with light lavender flowers. This particular plant is a favorite of many, but in recent years the lemon/rose fragrance so keenly described in the 1930s seems to be lacking from much of the stock available. It is a good garden specimen, and tolerates the dryness of most winter-heated homes with remarkably good grace.

'Rober's Lemon Rose' is a very long-lived cultivar. It does not train well as a standard because of its size and has a tendency to shoot off in odd directions. Grafted specimens are quite striking. It can be shaped as a topiary.

P. x *capitatum* 'Snowflake Rose'

This large plant is a good example of the difficulty faced in tracing down the ancestry of many of the scented cultivars. Some catalogs list it as *P. adcifolium*, which is a name of no botanical meaning. Old authorities list 'Scheidt's Ice Crystal Rose' and 'Both's Snowflake Rose'. Later books call the snowflake *P.* x *capitatum logii*.

It is an irregular form of the round-leafed rose, and may be splotched, streaked, or flecked with white. The variegation is probably due to a virus, since Snowflakes will revert to plain green leaves once they are grown in an optimum environment. By carefully selecting the most colorful cuttings, one can successfully propagate this rose-scented geranium through many generations. In the garden it will meander over a 4-foot circle in one season, although it seldom grows more than 20 inches high. It is a good basket plant, but unruly in a pot on the windowsill.

P. odoratissimum (Apple Geranium)

At last we come to a scented with a reasonable heritage. Scientists of the 1700s, including Linnaeus, L'Hertiers, and Aiton, knew of it and listed it in their works. A low-growing mound, the oval, almost rounded, pea-green leaves arise from a crownlike growth. Although not a true trailing geranium, the increasing diameter of the crown and the profuse white flowers borne on very long-stemmed growth make it an ideal hanging basket plant. Hang it in the breezeway and the gentle winds that turn and twist the basket help to release the fresh scent of apples. In the garden it will spread to an 18-inch circle, but because of its height it is at its best in a border.

Apples are easily grown from seed, but they readily cross-pollinate with others, particularly nutmeg. It is recommended that seed-bearing plants be isolated.

Cuttings should be made from the crown or from the nodes on the blooming stem. There are several delightful cultivars, and at least two different strains of old spice. One is more like the apple parent, the other favors the nutmeg side of the family. Both are pleasantly spicy.

P. x crispum 'French Lace'

Again, a scented with clear-cut lineage. This is sometimes called the 'Variegated Prince Rupert'. 'Prince Rupert', an old cultivar from the *P. crispum* group, appears on lists in the early 1800s. Like all the *crispums* the leaves of 'French Lace' are many, small, and tri-lobed; they are distinguished by narrow variegation. It is best to keep this one pinched to make it grow into a compact upright form. Otherwise it has a tendency to "grow informally," as one grower described it.

This elegant geranium requires more heat than its sire and

is subject to disease in cold or dampness. From the leaves come the clear scent of lemon. A very good pot plant, 'French Lace' surprises one with small, almost showy lavender flowers in midwinter. Water carefully when needed. It is at home in the garden, and prefers full sun and airy, breezy conditions.

P. citronellum 'Mabel Grey'

This handsome upright plant is more lemony than lemon. It was introduced to the United States from England in the 1970s via South Africa, according to one authority, although another says it came from Kenya. Whatever its origin, all gardeners should be glad it arrived. 'Mabel Grey' makes a wonderful standard because of its upright growth pattern. After much deliberation, it was placed on the International Registry of Geraniums in 1983 as a separate species. This was a great relief to many growers who were hard-pressed by their experiences and observations to accept 'Mabel Grey' as a mere hybrid of already known varieties.

The most successful cuttings are from the stem shoots. This treatment results in standards with incomparably sturdy stems that support a fragrant yellow-green ball. In midwinter it blooms with sudden beauty, a bright pink flower with carmine blotches and streaks.

Although more difficult to propagate than some other specimens, it has some resistance to cold, and several close relatives, such as 'Angel' and 'Frensham'. It is a collector's item, included here because of its desirability.

P. x radens 'Cinnamon Rose'

The deeply dentate, spicy, rose-scented green leaves of 'Cinnamon Rose' are easily distinguished from other dentate rose-scented varieties by the crisp, almost harsh, texture of the leaf, protruding veins, and the rows of cells rolled under at the edge of each leaf. There is much confusion about this nomenclature: some plants sold as Cinnamon may be incorrectly classified.

This particular Cinnamon Rose grows upright and rapidly in the garden and is unexcelled to train as a standard. In a year stems may be 24 inches tall, more than 1 inch in diameter, and supporting a ball of foliage 14 inches across. The leaves are excellent for use in jelly or syrup.

P. x *fragrans* (Nutmeg Geranium)

Another old favorite, long known and grown. Because of its similar size and shape, it is often linked with the apple. Although they are alike in many respects, such as their ability to cross-pollinate and their abundant small white flowers, apple and nutmeg are two distinct species. Nutmeg leaves are grey-green, soft, and lobed; the flowers are more distinctly marked with red splotches, and the stems are woody and branched. The sharp spicy fragrance may or may not resemble the smell of nutmeg, apparently depending on the way the plant is grown and the particular strain.

Good plants for borders, nutmegs bloom all summer in sunny open areas. They are attractive in hanging baskets, but three or more plants are required to produce a lush-looking display. They were much favored by the Victorians, who even wrapped sweet butter in nutmeg leaves for an unusual butter for tea sandwiches. This plant requires some care, since the lower leaves tend to become discolored. Variegated cultivars available include 'Snowy Nutmeg' (occasionally listed as 'Showy Nutmeg' or 'Golden Nutmeg'). The white variegation is not always a stable characteristic.

P. tomentosum (Mint Geranium)

Again, a clear-cut species, known and grown in cultivation for over 300 years. The very strong mint scent and huge velvety leaves make this a favorite in any collection. Garden specimens may grow to be 36 inches across, but mint geranium spreads laterally and is seldom more than 18 inches tall. It requires some shade for such a luxuriant display. The plant does well in large containers and does not demand the amount of water its size and texture would seem to require. It should be watered well when necessary, but overwatering results in yellowed leaves and soft growth.

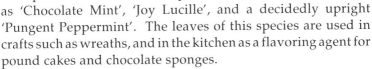

This has been crossed with others to produce such remarkable plants as 'Chocolate Mint', 'Joy Lucille', and a decidedly upright 'Pungent Peppermint'. The leaves of this species are used in crafts such as wreaths, and in the kitchen as a flavoring agent for pound cakes and chocolate sponges.

P. x *quercifolium* 'Fair Ellen'

The oak-leafed species has many cultivars, from the 'Giant Oak', which simply gallops over the ground in a garden, to the 'Village Oak', small and self-contained. 'Fair Ellen' falls somewhere in between. It has the deeply dentated and serrated leaves that distinguish all of the *quercifollii*, but its deep maroon center and veining add much interest. This is a profuse bloomer for a scented, with lavender blossoms tinged with carmine.

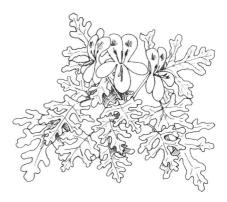

Although not as imposing as some of the family, this particular cultivar remains a favorite. The cool temperatures and long days of winter cause this plant to become leggy. In the house, however, it will produce abundant blossoms in December and January given adequate light. Strangely enough, all the *quercifolii* tolerate — in fact require — a good deal of water.

P. x *domesticum* 'Pink Champagne' et al.

This complex hybrid is known to have been crossed with one of the Martha Washington pelargoniums, themselves a complex cross. The 'Pink Champagne' is an unusual geranium, included because it is a vigorous plants with a striking pink blossom. No mention of it appears in any catalog until after 1960, so it is presumed to have been introduced in the last part of this century. On the other hand, it is quite possible it was known in the late 1800s under another name and has merely reemerged.

Because of its mixed breeding the plant should only be propagated from tip cuttings, and any seedlings or root growths ruthlessly destroyed — unless, of course, you want to spend several years trying to unravel its geneology.

So do enjoy these wonderful old-new plants. Don't pamper them. Pinch them when they become leggy, water them when they are dry, and groom them by removing yellowing leaves and spent flowers. They will reward you with wonderful odors, fascinating textures, luxuriant growth, and an insatiable desire to find new and different types.

Pelargonium Propagation

Once you have acquired a plant or two, you will want others. But the collector discovers that plants of like appearance may differ in their chief charm — scent. When you have found one you like, propagate it vegetatively — with cuttings — to assure that it will be duplicated. "Mother plants," as they are often called, should be strong and vigorous. Water them well several hours before taking cuttings. Cut "slips" 3 to 6 inches long with a very sharp knife or nurseryman's clippers, sterilized with alcohol. The best cuttings are from a stem that "snaps." Stems that bend may be soft and young, and those that refuse to snap are often woody. Both the very tender and the woody stems take longer to "strike," or produce roots.

Cut below an internode at an angle and remove lower leaves and stipules. Lay the cuttings out for 24 hours to "callus." This stimulates the growth of new cells — a callus — on the wound. Filtered light, a dry atmosphere, and no more than 70° F assures the best callusing. Placing cuttings in a frost-free refrigerator for 12 to 36 hours assures good callusing. It is not necessary to use a rooting hormone on geraniums. However, if you are going to root them in sand or soil, the fungicide contained in rooting compound may prove helpful.

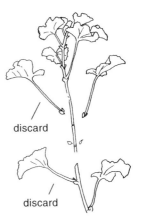

An old-fashioned pot-in-pot rooting bed is a time-honored way of rooting plant material. Use a large, broad, squat clay pot, a small clay pot, a small cork, and rooting medium of 1 part commercial growing mix and 1 part perlite, thoroughly mixed. Soak new pots overnight in water or thoroughly scrub old pots before using.

Put small pieces of nylon hose over the holes on the inside of the large pot. Fill loosely to within 1 inch of the top with damp rooting medium. Put a cork in the hole in the small pot. Scoop out the rooting medium in the center of the large pot and place the small pot firmly in the center of that hole, its rim even with or slightly above the rooting medium.

Stick the callused cuttings upright into the medium. Keep the corked, small pot filled with water. Put this nursery in a warm place in filtered light. In two weeks or so the cuttings will develop roots. Transplant to 3-inch pots using a commercial medium. When plants are growing vigorously, transplant again to a larger container or to the garden. Again, houseplant potting soil is not suitable for geraniums. A professional growing mix provides an optimum growing medium. See chart at

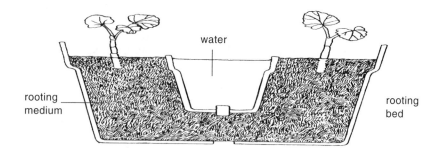

back of booklet for suggested mixes.
    Geraniums will root quite well in many other media such as clean sand or well-drained garden soil. Select a sheltered place in mottled shade in the garden. Remove soil or make a trench, and fill with ordinary sand. Make cuttings as described above and insert into the rooting bed, which should be kept damp. Check daily and remove wilted or discolored leaves or cuttings. Although the success rate is not so great, the use of small "cutting beds" is time-tested and can result in many beautiful plants.

Growing from Seeds

    Occasionally, scented pelargonium seeds are offered in a catalog. They may be quite good, or very ordinary, since hybridization occurs frequently. Gathering seeds from a rose-scented geranium you particularly favor is no guarantee that the resulting plants will be equally strong-scented. Wrap hanging baskets of nutmeg or apple in netting to capture the tiny, coiled, bristled seed and its nectar stem. If hanging baskets are isolated, or only one variety is grown, a true apple or nutmeg will result.
    Seed should be scattered on top of a very light, porous seed medium. As the spiral nectar tube absorbs water, it straightens out. This straightening movement acts something like a screwdriver, and the seed is screwed or drilled into the medium to the proper depth. The fresh seeds of many species germinate within ten to twelve days, although no exact figures are available for different cultivars.
    The cultivars have very diverse flower parts. Many of them

flower, but the pistil (female) may develop long after the stamens (male) have produced pollen and dried up. Some stamens produce only infertile pollen. Some stamens are very short, the minute amount of pollen they carry lost in the petals of the flower. Many seeds that develop are themselves infertile. This apparent lack of foresight on the part of Mother Nature may in fact be insurance that the stronger species and the better cultivars tend to survive.

Thus the surest way to propagate pelargoniums you wish to have multiplied is vegetatively with cuttings.

Decorative Uses

In the Landscape

The scented geraniums can be used effectively and uniquely in landscape design, with other herbs, with annuals, or in the perennial border. Several of the scenteds are continuous bloomers ('Fair Ellen', 'Staghorn Oak') and serve the same purpose as flowering annuals. However, in the Deep South they would be considered perennials.

In addition to the uprights for pots and the cascading plants for baskets, there are several vigorous cultivars that decisively command visual space. Their unusual texture and growth offer areas of contrast in mixed beds. The *quercifolium* species is especially good for such areas, as the oak-shaped leaves are quite different from the foliage of most bedding plants.

As specimen plants, surrounded by rock or mulch, the large-leafed oaks and the upright peppermint are eye-catching. It is pleasant to enjoy the beauty of flowering plants plus the aroma of the scented geraniums. You have added not only color and texture but intriguing odors to your garden scheme.

The velvety-leafed mint varieties prefer broken shade and do quite well in these areas as spreaders. Stressed in full sun, they flourish under trees and shrubbery. To use a new expression found in landscaping, they become "undercovers." Although tolerant to sun, the big-leafed roses of the *capitatum* species, such as 'Snowflake', 'Giant Rose', or 'Ruffled Leaf Rose', can also be utilized as undercover plants. They will grow well if they receive about six hours of sun a day.

Although not thought of as rock-garden plants, several of the smaller scenteds are good for such confined and restricted areas. Placed between rocks, the coconut, apple, nutmeg, 'Southernwood', and 'Attar of Rose' thrive. Many of the pelargoniums are good subjects for "xeriscaping," a term used to describe landscaping that does not require a great deal of water. With their deep roots, many varieties will cling tenaciously, even bloom frequently, in the most unlikely and unpromising of spaces. The cultivar 'French Lace' and others in the citrus-scented group adapt and flourish in a sunny, well-drained spot.

The scenteds are unique in that they provide that extra dimension of scent. This attribute is best utilized by having them in traffic areas where they will be brushed by garden visitors, or in a breezeway where the aroma can be wafted about by air currents. The hanging basket, patio container, or a large standard on either side of a formal door are all ways in which the scenteds can be used to emphasize, or adorn, a particular lifestyle.

In Containers

During the winter months, a south window filled with scenteds becomes an instant cure for winter doldrums. A 'Cinnamon Rose', trained as a standard, becomes a focal point, while pots of neat patterned 'Prince Rupert' or strawberry geranium can furnish accents as topiary subjects. Add a bonsai container or two of 'Southernwood' or 'Fingerbowl' for special interest and hang baskets with apple, nutmeg, or mint overhead. The window area becomes a delightful reminder of gardens yet to come.

To grow them well in containers a professional grower's mix is required; this is not to be confused with "potting soil." These professional mixes are available at a local nursery or garden center. Ordinary garden soil is not recommended for container growing, either on the patio or indoors. Most "potting soil" is designed for tropical houseplants and is too rich for the lusty geranium.

Select a container suitable for the cultivar. The apple, as has been suggested, does well in a hanging basket, but others that tend to sprawl about, such as 'Snowflake Rose', can also be used. The upright plants and rapid growers do better in large, heavy pots, preferably pots of clay or plastic pots weighted with either stone or brick.

The container you choose will depend on where you put your plant and the amount of time you feel you can devote to caring for it. Clay pots are ideal for that person who has a tendency to overwater, but if you don't have a lot of time, look for an attractive plastic pot (it takes less water and is more practical). If you like the look of clay, line the pot with plastic or paint the inside with paraffin wax (use old candles) to keep the water from evaporating.

Here is a trick for clay pots. Plant the geranium in a clay pot that will easily accommodate its roots. For the mint, 'Cinnamon Rose', or 'Pungent Peppermint' this means a 10-inch or larger container. Cover the drain hole of a container 2 inches larger with a piece of nylon, and put a 2-inch layer of peat or sphagnum moss in the bottom. Then insert the planted pot. Carefully fill in moss all around the inner pot, creating an insulating layer. When watered well, this additional layer will prevent the roots of the potted plant from becoming too dry or too hot in the noonday sun. If you go away for a weekend, place a saucer of water under the outer pot to assure the plant's well-being.

The scenteds with an upright habit are conversation pieces in a patio planter. A windowbox with a mixture of both upright and cascading types is an interesting experiment. Please consult the table at the end of this bulletin for information on varieties best suited for the different types of containers.

Your scented geraniums in containers will need to be fed. There are many different fertilizers to choose from: Peters Professional Soluble Plant Food offers a 20-20-20 general-purpose mix, which can be used twice a month with impunity. Osmocote, one of the slow-release fertilizers, especially the formulation 14-14-14, is ideal for planters and will last up to four months. This timed, controlled, or slow-release fertilizer (you will see all three words used to describe it) is composed of small granules of water-soluble nutrients. It can be mixed into your soil or top-dressed. These and others can be purchased from local garden stores.

Geranium Standards

Since the scented geraniums are fast-growing, they make good standards and topiaries. Results can be seen fairly quickly, and the satisfaction the grower receives in growing such a beautiful specimen is its own reward.

For the basic standard you will need: scented plant with a straight, unpinched leader, a bamboo or plastic stick to support the plant, plastic-coated ties, pot, and planting medium. Use a clay pot for stability or an ordinary nursery pot if you plan to conceal the container in a planter box. Fill the pot half full of medium, insert your support and the plant, and fill with growing medium. Tie the stem to the support at intervals to keep it straight. As the plant grows, remove the side shoots but do not pinch the leader until the plant reaches its ultimate height. Continue to remove tip growth from all small branches to induce more branching. Trim into a ball, or leave in a more natural shape. Just for fun, use three plants, braid the stems together, and form a single large head. The braided stem is attractive and very sturdy.

Topiary Forms

Topiary, meaning plants trimmed and trained into fantasy shapes, is another decorative use. Once you have collected a number of geraniums you will want to try your hand at creating one of these. There are all types. The scenteds can be trimmed into forms such as Christmas trees, spirals, and even animals. These plants do well in solariums or in southern exposure during the winter months. Scenteds with small leaves that grow rapidly are the best subjects for topiary forms. Again, please consult the chart at the end of the book for suggestions.

Bonsai

Of increasing interest is the Oriental art of bonsai. Traditionally, long-lived trees and shrubs are used for these forms. However, several of the scenteds mimic trees and shrubs, and can be trained as bonsai subjects. Because of their rapid growth it is possible to create an ancient-looking specimen in a few short months. The 'Southernwood', 'Fingerbowl', strawberry, and nutmeg have small leaves and woody stems that respond to the wiring, trimming, or weighting that produces a classic but "instant" bonsai display.

The scented geraniums have many decorative uses. As they continue to grow in popularity, more cultivars and sizes will be available, and those interested in the beautiful and unusual will want to explore the many ways of using them in the garden, on the patio, and in the home.

Crafting with the Scenteds

Potpourri

Not only are the scenteds fun to grow, but the flowers and leaves can be used in many crafts. Since the leaves smell so good, one of the first things to come to mind is how to preserve that aroma. Why not make your own special potpourri? In fact, our grandmothers always saved rose geranium leaves and roses to make sachets for dresser drawers each fall. When summer came again, out would go the old sachets, and fresh gleanings of scented leaves would once again be put in drawers and chests with linens, clothes, and keepsakes.

To harvest leaves, wait until the dew has dried. A late-morning or early-afternoon picking is best. Leaves will dry and maintain their green color if you gently cut them into small pieces with scissors, place them on a screen, and dry them in a dark place. They will dry faster and keep a better color if a fan is used to circulate the air. The leaves of the citrus, such as

'Mabel Grey', will dry yellow if left whole. A wonderful Christmas potpourri can be made from the pine and pungent-scented geranium leaves. Many of the *quercifolium* types of scented geranium leaves turn red when exposed to cold weather and will retain that red color when dried.

PINE FOREST POTPOURRI

2 cups scented geranium leaves
1 cup cedar chips
1 cup sassafras bark
⅛ dram oil (balsam or a pine)
1 cup hemlock cones
⅛ cup cloves
¼ cup cinnamon
1 cup basil flowers
1 quart red roses
1 cup crushed bay leaves
½ cup rosemary

Tussie-Mussies

Years ago the proper ladies of society carried a nosegay or a tussie-mussie. Nosegays were traditionally of sweet-scented flowers such as lavender, roses, and scented geranium leaves. Tussie-mussies included herbs as well, sometimes with special meanings, such as rosemary for remembrance. It was believed that this small fragrant bouquet would protect the bearer from infection and disease.

The ladies would make a tussie-mussie by starting with a single rose in the middle and surrounding it with lavender and rosemary, then smaller leaves of rose and lemon scenteds, and last, the large leaves of the mint-scented geranium. They would put it to their noses so they could not smell unpleasant odors. Tussie-mussies were also lovely accessories. Undoubtedly, they were used as were fans — as a means of flirting!

These bouquets were often dried and for sentimental reasons left on a desk, or amid the silver-handled combs and brushes on their dressing tables, as reminders of pleasant encounters. Sometimes they were dried and crumbled up to become a sachet.

Pressed Flowers

Many of us have cut a flower, a leaf, or a four-leaved clover and put it in a book, only to find it years later and marvel at how well preserved it is, thinking, why didn't I do more? The flowers of the scented geraniums are like tiny orchids and retain their vibrant colors even when dried. The leaves are so diverse in shape and texture that they are distinctively beautiful in a pressed flower picture.

Collect your leaves and flowers in the early afternoon. They should be completely free of dew but not faded or full-blown as they would be later in the day. Arrange them carefully on heavy blotting paper (do not use paper toweling; it has a texture that will imprint on the pressed material) or place them between layers of facial tissues. Put the prepared material in a flower press or between the pages of a heavy phone book or catalog. Be sure that the blossom or leaf is perfect, and that no corner or petal is turned or bent. Leave for a week or ten days. When they are dried and pressed, store between sheets of paper in a tight box or other container. A few spoonfuls of silica sand in the storage box absorb moisture and will help to retain the bright beauty you have captured.

Several good books offer directions and specifications for making pressed flower pictures. It is a Victorian art, now being revived, and one that many artists will find rewarding.

Pressed flowers and leaves are used on stationery and candles, and to decorate wedding invitations and birth announcements. A pressed leaf of 'Cinnamon Rose' makes a delightful Christmas card, since its shape is that of the Christmas tree. The uses for these delightful bits of scented color are as endless as a palette filled with paint.

Paper Making

Another art form being revived is that of making paper. The leaves of the scented geraniums add bulk and scent to the paper, while the tiny flowers add color. Kits are now appearing on the market for basic paper making, but many articles and ideas are available in books and in magazines.

It takes 2 cups of dried leaves to produce enough material to scent six to eight sheets of paper. A mere half-cup of blossoms will be more than enough to add colored flecks to the end product. Since the variables in this are so numerous, it will be up to the artisan to experiment with the scented geranium leaves and flowers. Those species and cultivars with large leaves and prominent veining are the most successful candidates for paper pulp.

Cooking with the Scenteds

The culinary uses of the scenteds are intriguing. Probably the best known is rose geranium jelly. Placing a single geranium leaf at the bottom of a jelly glass before pouring in apple jelly results in a delicately flavored rose jelly. Another scented geranium jelly recipe with a stronger flavor appears below.

SCENTED GERANIUM JELLY

1 quart apple juice or cider
2 cups fresh scented geranium leaves (rose, mint, or fruit)
5 cups sugar

Simmer leaves in apple juice 10 minutes. Remove leaves. Add a fruit pectin and bring to a full boil (one that cannot be stirred down). Add sugar and boil hard for 1 minute. Skim off with a metal spoon and pour into hot jars.

Judy Lewis, Lewis Mountain Herbs

Use this in hot tea over vanilla ice cream or puddings, or as a marinade for fruits.

ROSE GERANIUM SYRUP

2½ cups water
2 cups sugar
1 handful rose geranium leaves

Place water and sugar in a deep saucepan; stir until dissolved. Boil 5 minutes without stirring. Remove from heat, add rose geranium leaves, cover, and steep 10 minutes. Strain syrup into a clean pan and boil for 30 seconds. Remove from heat. Add a few drops of red coloring and pour into sterilized jars. Will keep 6 to 9 months in refrigerator.

Mary Peddie, Rutland of Kentucky

SCENTED GERANIUM SORBET

For a light, refreshing dessert, try this recipe. It's just the right touch after dinner.

2 cups sugar
5 cups water
¾ cups chopped lime- and lemon-scented geranium leaves

Place ingredients in saucepan and bring to a boil, stirring occasionally. When syrup reaches boiling point, reduce heat to low and simmer until thick (15 minutes), then freeze. While syrup is freezing, stir to break up ice crystals. The more you stir and refreeze, the smoother the sorbet. Serves four.

Cathy Renner, Rhamekins Herb Farm

SILVER SCENTED GERANIUM CAKE
This is from a famous restaurant in Cincinnati — a delightful cake.

¼ cup soft butter
¼ cup shortening
1⅓ cups sugar
2 teaspoons vanilla extract
3 unbeaten egg whites
2¼ cups cake flour
2½ teaspoons baking powder
¾ teaspoons salt
1 cup milk

Line a 9 x 12-inch pan with wax paper, then cover wax paper with scented geranium leaves ('Attar of Rose' for rose scent or 'Mabel Grey' for lemon scent). Set oven at 375°F. Cream butter and shortening with wooden spoon until smooth. Add sugar; stir in vanilla. Add egg whites and beat vigorously until fluffy. Add flour (sifted together with baking powder and salt) alternately with milk, ending with flour mixture and rest of milk. Pour into pan carefully. Bake 20 minutes or until done.

Janet Melvin, The Heritage Restaurant

When baking, poaching, or broiling fish, use finely chopped lemon- or lime-scented geranium leaves during the cooking process. The taste is superb.

Apple or rose-scented leaves added to the apples being cooked for applesauce adds distinctive flavor to the finished product.

Jeanne Rose, Noted Herbalist and Author

Kitchen Arts

The flowers of the scented geranium are edible. They can be incorporated into salads or hors d´oeuvres or served as a garnish. The leaves will flavor butters, honeys, and sugar. A leaf of 'Mabel Grey' in a goblet of ice water imparts the same freshness as a slice of lemon, only it is much more attractive. The foliage and flowers can be floated in punch. Make tea from 'Old-Fashioned Rose'. Try to combine the spice, mints, fruits, and rose together and make your own special blend of tea. A word of caution: Never use the pungent or pine-scented geraniums for teas or cooking, as they are too resinous to be tasty.

Revive an old custom: At your next dinner party use the tiny lemony leaves of the 'Fingerbowl' or 'French Lace' in fingerbowls. Or wrap a rose-scented leaf or 'Mabel Grey' leaf in a damp fingertip towel. Fold and put in a microwave 30 seconds or until heated thoroughly. A beautifully civilized way to offer your guests a thoughtful service!

The following chart is based on twenty years of observing, growing, and enjoying scented geraniums in zones 3, 4, 5, and 6. The category "Add Trace Elements" simply means that these particular species or cultivars do best with added minerals. Extra minerals can be added through additional fertilizers or by using blood meal, bone meal, or epsom salts in small quantities. Use only if the plants do not grow well, have yellow leaves, or otherwise evidence lack of vigor.

The required pH is for the most part neutral; however, a few varieties seem to grow better and bloom more frequently if they are occasionally fertilized with a slightly acid fertilizer. Even an occasional drink of cold tea or tea leaves scattered over the soil benefits these geraniums.

Growing & Usage Chart
Based on Garden Plants Grown in Zones 3, 4, 5, and 6

	Height	Ordinary Soil	Rich Loam	Add Trace Elements	pH	Border	Bedding Plant	Standard	Bonsai	Hanging Basket	Houseplant	Culinary Use	Potpourri	Topiary Subject
Attar of Rose	2'	X			N		X			X	X	X	X	
Skeleton Leaf Rose	4'	X		X	N		X	X			X		X	
Fern Leaf	3'	X		X	N		X				X		X	X
Nutmeg	18"	X		X	A	X				X	X	X	X	X
Rose, Capitatum	2'	X			N		X				X	X		X
Rose, Graveolens	3'	X			N		X				X	X	X	
Grey Lady Plymouth	3'	X			N		X				X	X	X	
Cinnamon Rose	4'	X			N		X	X			X	X	X	
Rober's Lemon Rose	4'	X		X	N		X				X		X	
Mint, Tomentosum	1'		X	X	N	X				X	X	X	X	
Ginger	2'	X		X	A		X				X		X	X
Southernwood	2'	X		X	N	X			X		X			X
Snowflake	2'	X		X	A		X			X	X		X	
Prince of Orange	2'	X		X	N		X					X	X	X
Fingerbowl	2'	X		X	N	X	X		X		X	X	X	X
French Lace	18"	X		X	A	X	X		X		X		X	X
Pink Champagne	3'	X			N		X	X			X	X		
Coconut	12"	X		X	N	X				X	X		X	
Lime	2'	X		X	N	X	X		X	X	X	X	X	X
Apple	1'	X		X	N	X				X	X	X	X	
Apricot	3'		X	X	A		X	X			X		X	
Strawberry	2'		X	X	N	X	X				X		X	X
Oak Leaf	3'	X			N		X	X			X		X	
Fair Ellen	2'	X			A		X			X	X		X	
Mabel Grey	4'		X	X	N			X			X		X	X